DEDICATION

This Coin Inventory Journal Log book is dedicated to all the Coin Collectors out there who love to collect coins and document their findings in the process.

You are my inspiration for producing books and I'm honored to be a part of keeping all of your Coin Inventory notes and records organized.

This journal notebook will help you record your details about your coins.

Thoughtfully put together with these sections to record: Sheet Number, Date, Quantity, Item Details, Description/ Mint/ Grade, Source, and Purchase Date & Price.

HOW TO USE THIS BOOK

The purpose of this book is to keep all of your Coin notes all in one place. It will help keep you organized.

This Coin Inventory Journal will allow you to accurately document every detail about your coins. It's a great way to chart your course through coin collecting.

Here are examples of the prompts for you to fill in and write about your experience in this book:

1. Sheet Number
2. Date
3. Quantity
4. Item Details
5. Description/ Mint/ Grade
6. Source
7. Purchase Date & Price

Enjoy!

COIN INVENTORY

Sheet no		Date	

QTY	ITEM	DESCRIPTION/MINT/GRADE	SOURCE	PURCHASE	
				DATE	PRICE

COIN INVENTORY

Sheet no	Date

QTY	ITEM	DESCRIPTION/MINT/GRADE	SOURCE	PURCHASE	
				DATE	PRICE

Coin Inventory

| Sheet no | | Date | | |

QTY	ITEM	DESCRIPTION/MINT/GRADE	SOURCE	PURCHASE	
				DATE	PRICE

COIN INVENTORY

Sheet no		Date		

| QTY | ITEM | DESCRIPTION/MINT/GRADE | SOURCE | PURCHASE ||
				DATE	PRICE

Coin Inventory

| Sheet no | | Date | | |

QTY	ITEM	DESCRIPTION/MINT/GRADE	SOURCE	PURCHASE DATE	PRICE

COIN INVENTORY

Sheet no		Date	

QTY	ITEM	DESCRIPTION/MINT/GRADE	SOURCE	PURCHASE	
				DATE	PRICE

Coin Inventory

Sheet no	Date

QTY	ITEM	DESCRIPTION/MINT/GRADE	SOURCE	PURCHASE DATE	PRICE

Coin Inventory

Sheet no	Date

QTY	ITEM	DESCRIPTION/MINT/GRADE	SOURCE	PURCHASE	
				DATE	PRICE

COIN INVENTORY		Sheet no	Date		PURCHASE	
QTY	ITEM	DESCRIPTION/MINT/GRADE	SOURCE		DATE	PRICE

Coin Inventory

| Sheet no | | Date | |

QTY	ITEM	DESCRIPTION/MINT/GRADE	SOURCE	PURCHASE DATE	PRICE

Coin Inventory

Sheet no	Date

QTY	ITEM	DESCRIPTION/MINT/GRADE	SOURCE	PURCHASE DATE	PRICE

COIN INVENTORY

Sheet no	Date

QTY	ITEM	DESCRIPTION/MINT/GRADE	SOURCE	PURCHASE	
				DATE	PRICE

Coin Inventory

Sheet no		Date		

QTY	ITEM	DESCRIPTION/MINT/GRADE	SOURCE	PURCHASE	
				DATE	PRICE

COIN INVENTORY

Sheet no	Date

QTY	ITEM	DESCRIPTION/MINT/GRADE	SOURCE	PURCHASE	
				DATE	PRICE

Coin Inventory

Sheet no		Date		

| QTY | ITEM | DESCRIPTION/MINT/GRADE | SOURCE | PURCHASE ||
				DATE	PRICE

COIN INVENTORY

Sheet no		Date	

QTY	ITEM	DESCRIPTION/MINT/GRADE	SOURCE	PURCHASE DATE	PRICE

Coin Inventory

Sheet no	Date

QTY	ITEM	DESCRIPTION/MINT/GRADE	SOURCE	PURCHASE DATE	PRICE

Coin Inventory

Sheet no	Date

QTY	ITEM	DESCRIPTION/MINT/GRADE	SOURCE	PURCHASE DATE	PRICE

COIN INVENTORY

Sheet no		Date	

QTY	ITEM	DESCRIPTION/MINT/GRADE	SOURCE	PURCHASE	
				DATE	PRICE

COIN INVENTORY

Sheet no: Date:

QTY	ITEM	DESCRIPTION/MINT/GRADE	SOURCE	PURCHASE	
				DATE	PRICE

Coin Inventory

Sheet no	Date

QTY	ITEM	DESCRIPTION/MINT/GRADE	SOURCE	PURCHASE DATE	PRICE

COIN INVENTORY

Sheet no	Date

QTY	ITEM	DESCRIPTION/MINT/GRADE	SOURCE	PURCHASE DATE	PRICE

COIN INVENTORY

Sheet no		Date		

| QTY | ITEM | DESCRIPTION/MINT/GRADE | SOURCE | PURCHASE ||
				DATE	PRICE

COIN INVENTORY

Sheet no		Date	

QTY	ITEM	DESCRIPTION/MINT/GRADE	SOURCE	PURCHASE	
				DATE	PRICE

Coin Inventory

Sheet no		Date		

QTY	ITEM	DESCRIPTION/MINT/GRADE	SOURCE	PURCHASE	
				DATE	PRICE

Coin Inventory

Sheet no		Date	

QTY	ITEM	DESCRIPTION/MINT/GRADE	SOURCE	PURCHASE	
				DATE	PRICE

Coin Inventory

Sheet no		Date		

QTY	ITEM	DESCRIPTION/MINT/GRADE	SOURCE	PURCHASE DATE	PRICE

Coin Inventory

Sheet no	Date

QTY	ITEM	DESCRIPTION/MINT/GRADE	SOURCE	PURCHASE DATE	PRICE

Coin Inventory

Sheet no		Date		

QTY	ITEM	DESCRIPTION/MINT/GRADE	SOURCE	PURCHASE DATE	PRICE

COIN INVENTORY

Sheet no:

Date:

QTY	ITEM	DESCRIPTION/MINT/GRADE	SOURCE	PURCHASE	
				DATE	PRICE

Coin Inventory

Sheet no:
Date:

QTY	ITEM	DESCRIPTION/MINT/GRADE	SOURCE	PURCHASE DATE	PRICE

COIN INVENTORY

Sheet no		Date	

| QTY | ITEM | DESCRIPTION/MINT/GRADE | SOURCE | PURCHASE | |
				DATE	PRICE

COIN INVENTORY

| Sheet no | | Date | |

QTY	ITEM	DESCRIPTION/MINT/GRADE	SOURCE	PURCHASE	
				DATE	PRICE

Coin Inventory

Sheet no		Date		

QTY	ITEM	DESCRIPTION/MINT/GRADE	SOURCE	PURCHASE	
				DATE	PRICE

Coin Inventory

Sheet no	Date

QTY	ITEM	DESCRIPTION/MINT/GRADE	SOURCE	PURCHASE DATE	PRICE

Coin Inventory

Sheet no		Date	

QTY	ITEM	DESCRIPTION/MINT/GRADE	SOURCE	PURCHASE DATE	PRICE

Coin Inventory

| Sheet no | | Date | | |

QTY	ITEM	DESCRIPTION/MINT/GRADE	SOURCE	PURCHASE DATE	PRICE

COIN INVENTORY

Sheet no	Date

QTY	ITEM	DESCRIPTION/MINT/GRADE	SOURCE	PURCHASE DATE	PRICE

Coin Inventory

Sheet no	Date

| QTY | ITEM | DESCRIPTION/MINT/GRADE | SOURCE | PURCHASE ||
				DATE	PRICE

COIN INVENTORY

Sheet no		Date		

| QTY | ITEM | DESCRIPTION/MINT/GRADE | SOURCE | PURCHASE ||
				DATE	PRICE

Coin Inventory

	Sheet no	Date

QTY	ITEM	DESCRIPTION/MINT/GRADE	SOURCE	PURCHASE	
				DATE	PRICE

Coin Inventory

Sheet no	Date

QTY	ITEM	DESCRIPTION/MINT/GRADE	SOURCE	PURCHASE DATE	PRICE

Coin Inventory

Sheet no:
Date:

QTY	ITEM	DESCRIPTION/MINT/GRADE	SOURCE	PURCHASE DATE	PRICE

Coin Inventory

Sheet no	Date

QTY	ITEM	DESCRIPTION/MINT/GRADE	SOURCE	PURCHASE	
				DATE	PRICE

Coin Inventory

Sheet no:
Date:

QTY	ITEM	DESCRIPTION/MINT/GRADE	SOURCE	PURCHASE DATE	PRICE

COIN INVENTORY

Sheet no		Date	

| QTY | ITEM | DESCRIPTION/MINT/GRADE | SOURCE | PURCHASE | |
				DATE	PRICE

Coin Inventory

Sheet no		Date		

QTY	ITEM	DESCRIPTION/MINT/GRADE	SOURCE	PURCHASE	
				DATE	PRICE

Coin Inventory

Sheet no		Date		

QTY	ITEM	DESCRIPTION/MINT/GRADE	SOURCE	PURCHASE	
				DATE	PRICE

COIN INVENTORY

Sheet no		Date		

QTY	ITEM	DESCRIPTION/MINT/GRADE	SOURCE	PURCHASE	
				DATE	PRICE

COIN INVENTORY

Sheet no	Date

QTY	ITEM	DESCRIPTION/MINT/GRADE	SOURCE	PURCHASE	
				DATE	PRICE

Coin Inventory

Sheet no		Date		

QTY	ITEM	DESCRIPTION/MINT/GRADE	SOURCE	PURCHASE	
				DATE	PRICE

Coin Inventory

Sheet no		Date		

| QTY | ITEM | DESCRIPTION/MINT/GRADE | SOURCE | PURCHASE ||
				DATE	PRICE

Coin Inventory

Sheet no		Date		

QTY	ITEM	DESCRIPTION/MINT/GRADE	SOURCE	PURCHASE	
				DATE	PRICE

COIN INVENTORY

Sheet no	Date

QTY	ITEM	DESCRIPTION/MINT/GRADE	SOURCE	PURCHASE DATE	PRICE

Coin Inventory

Sheet no:
Date:

QTY	ITEM	DESCRIPTION/MINT/GRADE	SOURCE	PURCHASE	
				DATE	PRICE

COIN INVENTORY

Sheet no		Date	

| QTY | ITEM | DESCRIPTION/MINT/GRADE | SOURCE | PURCHASE | |
				DATE	PRICE

Coin Inventory

Sheet no	Date

QTY	ITEM	DESCRIPTION/MINT/GRADE	SOURCE	PURCHASE DATE	PRICE

Coin Inventory

Sheet no		Date		

QTY	ITEM	DESCRIPTION/MINT/GRADE	SOURCE	PURCHASE	
				DATE	PRICE

Coin Inventory

Sheet no	Date

QTY	ITEM	DESCRIPTION/MINT/GRADE	SOURCE	PURCHASE DATE	PRICE

Coin Inventory

Sheet no		Date		

QTY	ITEM	DESCRIPTION/MINT/GRADE	SOURCE	PURCHASE	
				DATE	PRICE

Coin Inventory

Sheet no		Date		

QTY	ITEM	DESCRIPTION/MINT/GRADE	SOURCE	PURCHASE	
				DATE	PRICE

COIN INVENTORY

Sheet no:
Date:

QTY	ITEM	DESCRIPTION/MINT/GRADE	SOURCE	PURCHASE	
				DATE	PRICE

Coin Inventory

Sheet no:

Date:

QTY	ITEM	DESCRIPTION/MINT/GRADE	SOURCE	PURCHASE	
				DATE	PRICE

Coin Inventory

Sheet no	Date

QTY	ITEM	DESCRIPTION/MINT/GRADE	SOURCE	PURCHASE	
				DATE	PRICE

Coin Inventory

Sheet no	Date

QTY	ITEM	DESCRIPTION/MINT/GRADE	SOURCE	PURCHASE DATE	PRICE

COIN INVENTORY		Sheet no	Date			
QTY	ITEM	DESCRIPTION/MINT/GRADE	SOURCE	PURCHASE	
				DATE	PRICE

Coin Inventory

Sheet no		Date		

QTY	ITEM	DESCRIPTION/MINT/GRADE	SOURCE	PURCHASE DATE	PRICE

Coin Inventory

Sheet no	Date

QTY	ITEM	DESCRIPTION/MINT/GRADE	SOURCE	PURCHASE DATE	PRICE

Coin Inventory

Sheet no	Date

QTY	ITEM	DESCRIPTION/MINT/GRADE	SOURCE	PURCHASE DATE	PRICE

COIN INVENTORY

Sheet no	Date

QTY	ITEM	DESCRIPTION/MINT/GRADE	SOURCE	PURCHASE	
				DATE	PRICE

Coin Inventory

Sheet no	Date

QTY	ITEM	DESCRIPTION/MINT/GRADE	SOURCE	PURCHASE	
				DATE	PRICE

Coin Inventory

Sheet no	Date

QTY	ITEM	DESCRIPTION/MINT/GRADE	SOURCE	PURCHASE	
				DATE	PRICE

Coin Inventory

Sheet no	Date

QTY	ITEM	DESCRIPTION/MINT/GRADE	SOURCE	PURCHASE DATE	PRICE

COIN INVENTORY

Sheet no _____ Date _____

QTY	ITEM	DESCRIPTION/MINT/GRADE	SOURCE	PURCHASE DATE	PRICE

Coin Inventory

Sheet no		Date	

QTY	ITEM	DESCRIPTION/MINT/GRADE	SOURCE	PURCHASE	
				DATE	PRICE

Coin Inventory

Sheet no		Date	

QTY	ITEM	DESCRIPTION/MINT/GRADE	SOURCE	PURCHASE DATE	PRICE

Coin Inventory

	Sheet no	Date

QTY	ITEM	DESCRIPTION/MINT/GRADE	SOURCE	PURCHASE	
				DATE	PRICE

COIN INVENTORY

Sheet no	Date

QTY	ITEM	DESCRIPTION/MINT/GRADE	SOURCE	PURCHASE DATE	PRICE

Coin Inventory

Sheet no	Date

QTY	ITEM	DESCRIPTION/MINT/GRADE	SOURCE	PURCHASE DATE	PRICE

Coin Inventory

Sheet no		Date	

QTY	ITEM	DESCRIPTION/MINT/GRADE	SOURCE	PURCHASE	
				DATE	PRICE

Coin Inventory

Sheet no		Date				

| QTY | ITEM | DESCRIPTION/MINT/GRADE | SOURCE | PURCHASE | |
				DATE	PRICE

Coin Inventory

Sheet no	Date

QTY	ITEM	DESCRIPTION/MINT/GRADE	SOURCE	PURCHASE DATE	PRICE

Coin Inventory

Sheet no		Date		

QTY	ITEM	DESCRIPTION/MINT/GRADE	SOURCE	PURCHASE	
				DATE	PRICE

COIN INVENTORY

| Sheet no | | Date | |

QTY	ITEM	DESCRIPTION/MINT/GRADE	SOURCE	PURCHASE	
				DATE	PRICE

Coin Inventory

Sheet no	Date

QTY	ITEM	DESCRIPTION/MINT/GRADE	SOURCE	PURCHASE DATE	PRICE

Coin Inventory

Sheet no		Date		

QTY	ITEM	DESCRIPTION/MINT/GRADE	SOURCE	PURCHASE DATE	PRICE

Coin Inventory

Sheet no		Date		

QTY	ITEM	DESCRIPTION/MINT/GRADE	SOURCE	PURCHASE	
				DATE	PRICE

COIN INVENTORY

Sheet no		Date	

QTY	ITEM	DESCRIPTION/MINT/GRADE	SOURCE	PURCHASE	
				DATE	PRICE

Coin Inventory

Sheet no	Date

QTY	ITEM	DESCRIPTION/MINT/GRADE	SOURCE	PURCHASE DATE	PRICE

COIN INVENTORY

Sheet no	Date

QTY	ITEM	DESCRIPTION/MINT/GRADE	SOURCE	PURCHASE DATE	PRICE

Coin Inventory

Sheet no	Date

QTY	ITEM	DESCRIPTION/MINT/GRADE	SOURCE	PURCHASE DATE	PRICE

Coin Inventory

Sheet no		Date		

QTY	ITEM	DESCRIPTION/MINT/GRADE	SOURCE	PURCHASE	
				DATE	PRICE

Coin Inventory

Sheet no	Date

QTY	ITEM	DESCRIPTION/MINT/GRADE	SOURCE	PURCHASE DATE	PRICE

COIN INVENTORY

| Sheet no | | Date | |

QTY	ITEM	DESCRIPTION/MINT/GRADE	SOURCE	PURCHASE	
				DATE	PRICE

Coin Inventory

Sheet no	Date

QTY	ITEM	DESCRIPTION/MINT/GRADE	SOURCE	PURCHASE DATE	PRICE

COIN INVENTORY

Sheet no	Date

QTY	ITEM	DESCRIPTION/MINT/GRADE	SOURCE	PURCHASE	
				DATE	PRICE

Coin Inventory

Sheet no	Date

QTY	ITEM	DESCRIPTION/MINT/GRADE	SOURCE	PURCHASE DATE	PRICE

COIN INVENTORY

Sheet no		Date		

| QTY | ITEM | DESCRIPTION/MINT/GRADE | SOURCE | PURCHASE ||
				DATE	PRICE

Coin Inventory

Sheet no	Date

QTY	ITEM	DESCRIPTION/MINT/GRADE	SOURCE	PURCHASE DATE	PRICE

COIN INVENTORY

Sheet no		Date	

| QTY | ITEM | DESCRIPTION/MINT/GRADE | SOURCE | PURCHASE | |
				DATE	PRICE

Coin Inventory

Sheet no: Date:

QTY	ITEM	DESCRIPTION/MINT/GRADE	SOURCE	PURCHASE DATE	PRICE

COIN INVENTORY

Sheet no | Date

QTY	ITEM	DESCRIPTION/MINT/GRADE	SOURCE	PURCHASE DATE	PRICE

Coin Inventory

Sheet no	Date

QTY	ITEM	DESCRIPTION/MINT/GRADE	SOURCE	PURCHASE	
				DATE	PRICE

COIN INVENTORY

Sheet no		Date		

QTY	ITEM	DESCRIPTION/MINT/GRADE	SOURCE	PURCHASE	
				DATE	PRICE

Coin Inventory

Sheet no		Date		

QTY	ITEM	DESCRIPTION/MINT/GRADE	SOURCE	PURCHASE	
				DATE	PRICE

Coin Inventory

Sheet no:

Date:

QTY	ITEM	DESCRIPTION/MINT/GRADE	SOURCE	PURCHASE	
				DATE	PRICE

www.ingramcontent.com/pod-product-compliance
Lightning Source LLC
Chambersburg PA
CBHW071402080526
44587CB00017B/3153